Cherish Her

Cherish Your Self! ♡

By Garry Cale

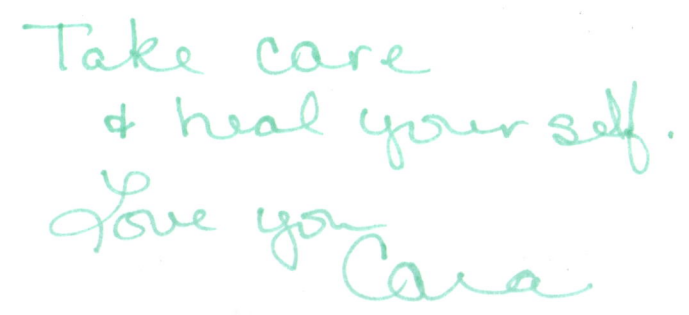

Take care
& heal yourself.
Love you
Cara

High Point Publications • Olympia, WA 98507-2629

Copyright © 2005 by High Point Publications
Front Cover © 2005 by Shawna Hansen
Edit by Mary Musick and Kristy Turner
Library of Congress Catalog Number: 2002117592
ISBN: 0-9727743-0-0

All rights reserved, which include the right to reproduce this book or any portions thereof in any form whatsoever except as provided by the U.S. Copyright Law. For information address High Point Publications, P.O. Box 2629, Olympia, WA 98507-2629.

Printed in the United States of America

Publication Date: February 2005

FIRST EDITION

Table of Contents

Dedication i

Introduction iii

Cherish and Respect Women 1

Cherish Wives 15

Cherish Her with Romance 25

Cherish Her by Showing Her She's Special 35

Cherish Mothers 43

Cherish Sisters 49

Cherish Daughters 55

Final Thoughts 67

Dedication

This book is dedicated to the *special women* who have graced my life. While I cannot name all of these wonderful women, I will mention a few. First, I will mention Cathy with whom I have shared many wonderful years. You were good for me. (Thank you!) Second, my daughter Karen brings joy to my days with her smile and energy. Both of you have been among my greatest blessings.

Thanks should be extended to my mother (Betty Cale) and aunt (Donnie McQuater) who always said, "I want you to grow up and be a nice young man." My sister (Terressa Cale Jackson) should be mentioned because she gives the best hugs and she is a loving person.

I want to thank my first grade teacher (Evelyn Williams) who gave me a dream to attend college. "Yes, I got my college degree." I also want to thank my aunt (Josephine Thomas) who talked to me when I had questions about young ladies. I also want to thank every woman with whom I have shared a friendship, a smile, a joke, a meal, a tear, laughter, love and our hearts and spirits.

Dedication

This book is also dedicated to my dad (Robert Cale) and my uncles (Thomas McQuater and William Thomas.) I watched you and tried to duplicate the attention that you gave to the women in your lives. "Yes, I was paying close attention."

Special thanks are extended to my friend, Martha Roach. She looked inside of me and saw this love that I have for treating women in special ways and told me I should share my wisdom with others. I consider her the catalyst behind this book. I also need to thank two dear friends (Kristen Abbott and Diane Marks) who listened to my ideas and were instrumental in selecting the title and encouraging me until completion.

Most importantly, I would like to thank my Creator who gave me a good spirit, a loving family, and a good church (Rogers Memorial Baptist Church in Knoxville, TN). Yes, I have been blessed; and now, I will share with you the love that I have extended to the women of my life in ***Cherish Her.***

Introduction

Writing this book has brought me immense joy. It has provided an opportunity to share with you some of the most important people in my life and our special relations. And while I do not profess to be an expert in relationships, I have had the privilege of sharing time, conversation, smiles, hugs, tears, laughter and joy with special women.

"Have I lived a charmed life and these women always been perfect in my eyes?" I answer by saying, "I am living a wonderful life and the women I describe in *Cherish Her* make it more exciting. They add a zest that allows my happiness to be taken to another level."

My intentions for writing *Cherish Her* are quite simple: 1) I want to thank the special women in my life for their contributions, 2) I would like to share with you how I have displayed my appreciation and thanks for their generous spirits, and 3) lastly, I would like to generate creativity in others so that they can develop a healthy behavior that is respectful of women.

Cherish and Respect Women

Every morning when I talk to My Creator,
I thank My Creator for the special women in my life.

I ask My Creator to keep these special women safe and to watch over them.

I ask My Creator to give them strength and empower them throughout the day.

I ask My Creator to bless each one individually, collectively and in a very special way!

I also pray for my strength so that I may be a better man, husband, father, son, nephew and friend to these special women.

Cherish and Respect Women

Choose good words when you speak to her!
("You are a wonderful person!" "It is a pleasure to see you!"
"I am blessed to share your love!" "Or simply say "Please." when requesting her help and "Thank you!" after receiving her assistance.")

⁂

Respect her opinions! Give her the respect you want when speaking.
(It's her opinion, even though you may not agree. Listen patiently without interrupting. Don't get defensive if she disagrees with you. This isn't a competition; it's a sharing of ideas.)

⁂

Respect every woman you date and enjoy her company; she has the potential to be your wife for life.

❧

Learn to love yourself. Love yourself more than anyone or anything in this world. Accept yourself, including every little imperfection. Once you are able to love yourself in this manner, you can love and give to her without question.

❧

Cherish and Respect Women

When you make a list of your goals or dreams, talk to her about her desires. Together, build a plan that will assist both of you in the accomplishment of mutual goals.

❧

While she is asleep or during a quiet moment, take some time to just devour her with your eyes.
(Take in her beauty; her eyes, hair, shoulders, curves and all the special things that make her wonderful in your eyes.)

❧

Compliment the obvious! Take notice of her. Speak up. Sincere compliments are always good.
("You look beautiful today!" or "Is that outfit new? You make it look wonderful!" "Is that a new hairdo? Your hairstyle accentuates your natural beauty!")

Behind every great woman is an outstanding man!
(Sometimes, he's out standing in the cold. Support her dreams and goals.)

❧

Don't let the woman of your life walk away from you without sharing a piece of your heart or mind!
(Tell her, "I am interested in you and I want to discover who you are!" Or "I would like to share some of your time over a latte or glass of wine!")

❧

Do the special things to keep her that you did to get her!
(Did you send her flowers, give nice cards, write poetry, go out on dates or take her to dinner? Do you still send her flowers, buy nice cards, write poetry for her, take her to dinner or go out on dates?)

Compliment the not-so-obvious and seldom-mentioned things you appreciate!
("I appreciate you keeping the checking account for us." or "Thank you for listening to me discuss my day!" or "I appreciate you cooking for us!" It may sound old fashioned, but she will appreciate it.)

❧

Seek opportunities by which you and she can contribute to help others. Work together and grow closer by blessing others.

❧

Savor the moments you spend with her by capturing the special days on film or video, and revisit your photo albums regularly. These treasures will open your eyes and show you how much you really care for her.

Remember, if you respect her, in most cases, she will reciprocate and respect you.

🥀

Relationships are built on trust. It is the foundation of similar beliefs, respected integrity and most often, an unspoken principle.
(In new relationships, make sure the unspoken principle is communicated to each other.)

🥀

All life is a gift. The life she shares with you is her gift to you. The life you share with her is your gift to her. Cherish her through the good times as well as the not so exciting or painful times because life is precious.

Cherish and Respect Women

Encourage her to enjoy her friends. It can also be a good time for you to plan an outing with your children or friends, watch a movie, or enjoy one of your pet projects or hobbies without interruption.
(When she returns, ask her, "How are your friends?" or "Did you and your friends have a good time?")

❧

Never put her friends down or make negative comments. Making such comments suggests that she is not a good judge of character. Remember she chose you.

❧

Humble yourself! Admit when you are wrong!
(OK! OK! This one isn't easy. This doesn't mean you have to grovel. Simply saying, "I'm not always perfect or right!" is a true fact.)

Never forget her birthday!
(She may tell you that it is okay, but your forgetfulness hurts her deeply. Her friends will ask, "What did he give you for your birthday?" Remember, she wants to impress them by telling them how thoughtful and sweet you are!)

❧

Three delightful keys to a Woman's Heart are:

- ◆ Flowers
- ◆ Chocolate
- ◆ Ice Cream

❧

Focus on her everyday and learn something new about her. I've found daily joy as I grow closer and give my time, energy and attention to the women in my life.

When she wants to talk, turn off the television.
(You can record the program to watch later. Give her your undivided attention.)

❧

When she wants to talk with you about a problem at work or about friends, don't attempt to solve it unless she asks. Just listen.

❧

I found that when women want to talk to you about a problem, they want you to listen. Most of the time, they are not looking for men to solve the problem, but they want men to do the other part of communication; listen. *(She wants you to be a sounding board; not a knight in shining armor who rides in to save the damsel who is stressed.)*

If she locks her keys in the car and she calls you for help, be a hero! Rescue her and tell her, "I am glad that I can be the one you call."

- ♦ Rush to her side.
- ♦ Unlock her car.
- ♦ Tell her, "I'm glad you called me."

(Never be critical of the incident. She already feels embarrassed, has already criticized herself and probably called you as the last resort. When you're around others, don't mention the incident. She'll thank you later.)

☙

Revel in the warmth of her heart and kindness of her spirit. Appreciate the wonder of her touch, the beauty in her eyes and melody of her voice. Thank your Creator for her; for the Creator is good!

When you travel and you are away from home, call her to let her know you have arrived safely and say that you miss her.
(If you have an opportunity, buy a small gift to let her know you were thinking about her and present it to her upon your return. Do not forget to tell her how much you missed her.)

☙

Share your intentions and desires with her as you start to think about expanding your horizons like pursing a new job in another city, changing apartments or visiting family/friends out of town. She will appreciate you keeping her informed.

Cherish and Respect Women

Women were created for more than just a desire for physical beauty. Don't be afraid to dig deep and discover a treasure in her inner beauty.
(You might find a more wonderful person than you noticed at first glance.)

❧

Always treat a woman with respect during your relationship with her.
(I always treat a woman like I want my sister to be treated. I believe my sister deserves to be treated in a first class manner; with dignity and respect.)

❧

When time permits, tell female co-workers when they have done a good job.
(Everyone deserves to be recognized. Sometimes, the most outwardly confident person is also nervous and has doubts of her abilities.)

Cherish Wives

Wives are special women with whom you share a lifetime of joy, dreams and happiness. Wives give love that satisfies and stimulates their husbands.

Wives help raise their husbands' levels of accomplishment within their relationships. Wives also compliment their husbands' strengths, and help them compensate for any weakness.

Every wife is beautiful because her spirit longs to be with his, making both of your spirits one; united in this world. In union there is strength. She will add power and balance to your life.

A wife is priceless:

- She is soulmate; she will grow to understand your heart and its desires.
- She is mother; she will birth your children and assist in carrying your legacy into the future.
- She is confidante; she will encourage you to pursue your greatest dreams and support you when doubts arise. **She is wife.**

When a man marries a woman, she becomes his leading lady. The love they share is stronger than the love of parents and siblings because your spirits become united. Together, they will build a future and always be in each others hearts and dreams.

❧

The beginning of a life as a married couple is not farewell to being single; it's the beginning of a new dynasty with interesting adventures and realities for you to discover.

❧

Start your marriage with trust, hope and dreams. Let faith be the musical instrument that guides you as you work to build your trust, maintain hope through the ups and down, and work toward attaining your dreams.

Treat her mother respectfully. Never make negatives comments about her.
(Just remember, your wife has some of the same genes as her mother. It is better to question than to make a statement such as, "Why does your mother always bake apple pie for dessert?" This allows you to be in the discovery mode versus the criticizing mode.)

༄

Before you make large purchases like a car, boat, jet ski, or riding lawn mower be sure to let her know your intentions. She may want to discuss the budgeting aspect. Most of all, she will appreciate you keeping her informed.

༄

When you and your wife agree upon a plan of action, make sure you execute your part of the agreement.
(If you have doubts or change your mind, always talk to her <u>before</u> the deadline.)

Winning isn't everything! Relationships are partnerships and a united team effort is always stronger than a divided one.
(In competition, when there is a winner, there is a loser. Try to create win-win situations for both of you. This means both partners should be willing to compromise.)

༄

Remember: Only your wife can honestly say whether or not you are a good husband. *(It doesn't matter what people outside of your relationship think or say. Always give her your best.)*

༄

Make plans and <u>be flexible</u> throughout your marriage.
(Sometimes the needs of the family, sales at the mall or a mothering instinct of newborns can change the most well-crafted plans.)

With her assistance, create a comfortable home for both of you and your children, filled with warmth and love that welcomes family and friends.

❧

Every month, add an extraordinary experience to your life. These extraordinary experiences may include a new taste of ice cream, a new recipe, a picnic, visit a new park, a museum, a new restaurant, attendance of a play, concert, sporting event or car show.

❧

Once in a while, you need to be impulsive toward her.
(Give her a call when you think about her during the day. Ask her for a lunch date. After she has had a long day, give her a neck massage to relieve stress and tension.)

Marriage is a union. Each partner should have a special interest in making it successful. Each partner should give to make the union strong.
(Write down the special things that you will bring and want to accomplish in your marriage. After you both have a list, discuss them. Did you discuss money, children, careers, where you want to live and decision-making?)

❧

Marriage is like a bouquet of flowers; each day is like a flower blooming and it grows more wonderful as each day of marriage unfolds.
(Sometimes, people get so busy that they don't make time to enjoy the excitement of family. Then one day, they notice that their children are about to graduate and leave home. And they start to think, "Where did the time go?")

Find an activity or event she likes that you can also enjoy.
(I discovered my wife likes baseball and college basketball. Going to a baseball game is a nice date or good family outing!)

෴

The most romantic gifts that you can give to a woman are time and feeling.
(If they know that you took time to search and deliberate over a gift for them, they are often pleased. The gift doesn't always have to be expensive to be special.)

෴

Sometimes, life is unpredictable. Be aware that no one always makes the right choices. Be forgiving and when your turn comes, she will be also.
(In your marriage, leave room for the unexpected and learn from these experiences.)

Cherish Wives

Marriage is like riding a roller coaster; when you see it from a distance it can look scary and awesome. When you experience it, you suddenly realize that it was worth the journey and much, much more.

❧

Carry a token of your love for your wife.
(When you're away from home, look at it and know that she is with you always.)

❧

Tell her, "I love you!"
(Tell her often and let your actions speak louder than these words.)

Love your wife and create loving memories for her and both your daughters and sons. It's said that you only go around once in life, therefore, "Live your life with gusto!"

❧

Discover how she celebrates special days. Discuss how you also celebrate them. Together, build a successful formula for celebrating these special days.

❧

Plan a vacation together. Make sure you include a little adventure for the family, a little alone time for romance, and a lot of togetherness for the family.

Cherish Her with Romance

Romance is a full body experience to be shared. *Romance* requires you to open the creativity of your mind and the passion of your heart. *Romance* requires vision, emotion and flexibility. *Romance* is best experienced when your five senses are fully stimulated.

Romance creates laughter and feels like you are on a journey to a magical place. *Romance* with someone can take on mystery, adventure and fun. *Romance* may include love or simple fun.

Romance can be intoxicating, but is never forced. *Romance* can be simple words, actions or deeds, but always involves thoughts that are selfless. *Romance* her often and well.

Cherish Her with Romance

Set the mood for romance! While cooking dinner, set the table with the good china. *(Don't forget to add candles and soft music! Wear a dash of your favorite cologne that she bought you and walk by her so that she can smell it's fragrance.)*

❧

Record the favorite song that brought you together. Take time to dance with her in the den or living room. *(Ask her, "May I have the honor of this dance?")*

❧

From time to time, play this song that ignited the love flame between you. From time to time, hum or sing this loving tune to let her know you haven't forgotten.

Get in touch with her five senses by sharing the following:

- *Purchase a bouquet of flowers or special perfume.*
- *Visit a museum or view a waterfall.*
- *Rise early one spring morning and listen to the birds sing.*
- *Order a different menu item the next time you dine out.*
- *Give each other a back massage with scented oils or lotions.*

ॐ

When you're walking together, reach out and hold her hand. Squeeze it gently, and pause occasionally to look into her eyes.

ॐ

At least once a week, hold her in your arms and give her a two minute hug. *(Okay, for beginners, you can start with a 30 second hug.)*

Cherish Her with Romance

Create and plan an evening for romance. Place a couple of logs in the fireplace to create warmth. Set the table with an arrangement of flowers that add aroma to the ambiance and beauty to the table. Set the table with the good china and crystal. Serve her dinner and don't forget dessert.

ಸಿ

When she arrives home from work, take her jacket and remove her shoes while placing slippers on her feet. Ask her to sit down and pour her a chilled glass of her favorite wine, sparkling champagne, cider or beverage.

ಸಿ

Let her enjoy her beverage while dinner is being prepared. Serve her with a tray of appetizers. *(Include cheese, crackers, grapes, strawberries or shrimp cocktail.)*

Have the dinner catered (by a friend) or cook a quick delicious meal.
(Personally, I like Sicilian steak, baked potatoes and a broccoli casserole. See recipes at the end of this chapter.)

❧

Always thank her! Always thank her and complete the thank you with:

- Her name;
- Terms of endearment such as love, sweetheart, honey or baby; or
- Nickname.

❧

Acknowledge her when she walks into the room.
(Stand up and take her hand!)

❧

Every now and then, you need to count the ways she has added joy, laughter, happiness and other blessings to your life.

Cherish Her with Romance

They say chivalry is dead, but I found out that it is the best way to go:

Open car and building doors for her. Help her sit down at restaurants. Walk on the outside of the sidewalk. When it's raining, shield her from the rain with your umbrella. *(Of course, I have lived in Washington State where it rains almost every week.)*

&

When you're washing your cars, wash her car <u>first</u>.
(Be sure to clean the interior and dry the car.)

&

Ask her to order dinner first by saying, "Why don't you order first?" or simply ask, "May I order dinner for the two of us?" Be sure you have eaten at this restaurant and know what she likes before you attempt to order her meal.

Valentine's Day is for candy, flowers and a Valentine's Day card.

❧

Give her your special look; the look that says, "I love you!"

❧

When you say you love her, trust her! With all of your heart, trust her!

❧

Treasure her by giving her your best, putting her needs above others and showing her she is special. Let your heart overflow with good thoughts and actions toward her.

Recipes:

<u>Sicilian Steak</u>

2 steaks (New York or T-bone)   Italian Caesar dressing
Garlic powder   Black Pepper

In large bowl, pour dressing to cover steaks. Sprinkle at least 1 teaspoon of garlic powder and half the amount of black pepper. Cover and marinate for at least ½ hour. (The longer you marinate, the better the seasoning.)

Cook steaks on grill for 8-10 minutes on each side at medium high temperature for medium-well doneness.

Broccoli Casserole

2-10 oz. packages of chopped broccoli
1 tablespoon of light mayonnaise
¼ cup of chopped cheddar cheese

1 can cream of mushroom soup
1 tablespoon lemon juice
3-4 crushed saltine crackers

Preheat oven to 350 degrees. Thaw broccoli and drain. Place in 1 quart cook pan. Add soup, mayonnaise, lemon juice, stirring together. Place cheese throughout mixture. Sprinkle crackers on top of mixture. Bake uncovered for 30 minutes or until mixture is bubbly around edges.

Baked Potato

Wash and dry potatoes. Prick potatoes with a fork. Microwave 6-10 minutes until desired doneness is achieved.

Strawberry Cloud Pie

2 graham cracker pie crusts (fat-free)
6 oz. Strawberry Jell-O gelatin
8 oz. Cool Whip Lite
4-6 medium strawberries
1 banana (optional)

Make Jell-O according to instructions on box. Place Jell-O in refrigerator and let it set for approximately 1½ hours until it is not runny, but not totally solid. Dice four strawberries. Remove Jell-O from the refrigerator and scoop cool whip into bowl with Jell-O. Use a hand mixer and whip both cool whip and Jell-O approximately two minutes at medium speed. (Make sure it is well mixed, but not pureed.) Fold in diced strawberries with spoon.

Spoon Jell-O mixture into pie crusts. Cover and place in refrigerator for at least four hours or overnight. Before serving, slice strawberries lengthwise and place atop of each pie. When serving, you may serve banana slices with each slice of pie. Enjoy!

Cherish Her by Showing Her She's Special

Anytime you are involved in a relationship with a young lady or a woman, it is imperative that you let her know that she is special. There are many reasons why you are attracted to her. Sometimes you can tell her why, and other times it is very hard to put into words.

Therefore, when you come up short in the vocabulary department, it is far easier to display your attraction to her through thoughtful actions, pleasant conduct and tasteful manners. (This can be as easy as remembering special days or using table manners.)

Treating her nicely and respectfully is endearing. Greeting her with a big smile or a gentle hug often means more than words. In an exclusive way, it says, "You are special to me!"

Cherish Her by Showing Her She's Special

Plan special activities for her birthday, Christmas and your anniversary!
(Give her "special" flowers, a loving card, and a gift or treat her to dinner!)

❧

Assist her with her coat or jacket.
(Hold her coat lower than the back of shoulders. Allow her to put one arm in at a time. Lift the coat as both arms are inserted. Lift her hair off her shoulders to allow the collar of her coat to be placed under her hair.)

❧

Put your arm around her while you're watching television or a movie.
(Look into her eyes and say, "I'm enjoying spending time with you.")

Take the time to kiss her when you depart her company!
(Take her in your arms, look into her eyes and plant a kiss on her that says, "I can't wait to see you again." Then give her a hug, softly, gently, but firmly.)

❧

Take her to a movie that she wants to see. Purchase the tickets in advance to avoid waiting in a long line.

❧

Take her to her favorite restaurant. Make reservations and ask for a table with a view that will add sparks to your conversation. Arrange for a small bouquet of flowers to be on the table with a note from you.

Cherish Her by Showing Her She's Special

Buy her gift certificates to her favorite store, spa, restaurant or boutique.

☙

Be responsible for dinner at least two nights a week. Plan and prepare a full, balanced meal. *(Only preparing the main course does not add up to a full, balanced meal.)*

☙

Always give her something special for her birthday!
(Start gathering information from her friends months in advance. Months before her birthday, ask her to go to the local mall when you need to purchase some items. Make mental notes when she stops to window shop. <u>I always avoid giving gifts that require her to work such as a washing machine, vacuum cleaner or sewing machine</u>.)

When you're invited to her place for dinner, arrive on time (**never early**) with a small bouquet of flowers or a chilled bottle of wine or sparkling cider.

❧

The moment you notice how beautiful she looks, tell her. When you start to think about her outside of her presence, tell her. When you start enjoying her companionship, see her more often and tell her.

❧

When you plan a romantic evening, **make sure the focus is on her**. Select the restaurant or food she likes. Make sure the conversation is about subjects that interest her. Avoid going to places where your friends go or where you will be interrupted often.

Cherish Her by Showing Her She's Special

Find ways to thank her for an exciting evening. Give her a call and tell her you had a fantastic time. Send flowers the next day or purchase a small gift such as votive candles.

❧

Find ways to include her as you take care of yourself.
(When you take your laundry to the dry cleaners, take hers too. Pick up her laundry from the cleaners.)

❧

Take her breakfast in bed. Make sure the breakfast includes healthy foods, a napkin and water or juice. Bring the morning newspaper for her to read.
(As she eats, sit beside the bed and have light conversation with her. Tell her that you just want to show that you appreciate her.)

Cherish Her by Showing Her She's Special

Send flowers to her workplace or to her parents' home while she's visiting them. *(Write a little note to send with the flowers with nothing less than "Thinking of You!" This shows you took the time to select the flowers and sign the card as opposed to merely telephoning the order to a local florist.)*

❧

Create unique ways to thank her for a special date or evening.
*(Mail a handwritten note the next day. Give her a candy jar filled with her favorite candy. Send her balloons or a heart-shaped cookie for a **special** touch!)*

❧

Invite her to have brunch on a weekend; it's a nice change of pace.

❧

If you ever want to make her very happy, tell her, *"This is just between you and me. Tell me exactly what it will take to please you or one goal you want to accomplish. And I will sacrifice and help create the opportunity for you to achieve it."*

Cherish Mothers

Mothers are the givers of life. Mothers inherently established the first bond with their babies. During the term of each pregnancy, mothers provide a place to sleep, feed and care for their unborn babies. Mothers endure nausea, restless nights, increased weight gain, numerous trips to bathrooms and oftentimes, a painful foot in the ribs when an unborn baby is a little fidgety.

Mothers are daunting. If you've not witnessed the birth of a child, you can never understand what your mother endured. The birthing of a child is one of the most blessed events of life because it is the beginning of a life on earth.

Mothers are priceless. Mothers often give their time and energy for their family until they reach a state of exhaustion. Mothers deserve our praise.

Cherish Mothers ─────────────────────

To a Father, a son grows up and becomes a man.
However, to a Mother, a son is always her little boy.
(My mother still blows me kisses as we finish our telephone calls.)

❧

Be grateful to your Mother; she carried you before the world saw you.
(Morning sickness, extra weight and uncomfortable days were endured for you.)

❧

Mother's Day is a time of action for you!
Send her those *special* flowers and give her a call.
(She'll rave about the flowers and tell her friends so they will be envious.)

A Mother is not perfect in the way she raises you; she's human. Just remember, you didn't come with an owner's manual.
(I thought my mother didn't understand me, until I realized that she had donated only half of my genes.)

❧

<u>Never</u> forget your Mother's birthday!
It will help you remember special days for important women in your life.

❧

Ask your mother to teach you how to cook simple meals, sew on buttons and take care of laundry. These skills will benefit you after you leave her home and far into the future.
(She will be happy to tell her friends how well you can take care of yourself.)

Honor and respect your Mother and Father. It is a monumental task to be a parent and the pay scale is low for the twenty-four hour care they provide. I believe the respect you show will add years to your life.

❧

Forgive your mother for any motherly things she says or displays around your friends, girlfriends, children or wife.
(Mothers will bring out old photo albums or tell stories that will make you want to crawl under a rock or make you feel proud as a peacock.)

❧

Mothers *may* offer their opinion about women you date. Most assuredly, they ***will*** give opinions about a future wife, their daughter-in-law.
(I assure you that they have your best interest at heart. They want to see you date or marry a loving person.)

Take the best qualities you see in your mother and make sure that you find a woman to marry who has those qualities and more.
(Surprisingly, men like consistent behavior. The one woman that men are most familiar and comfortable with is their mother.)

☙

As your mother matures, be aware that she may need your assistance.
(Call her and offer your services or arrange for support.)

☙

Ask your mother to talk about her family. Discover the history of her heritage and unlock the family secrets. Discover how your parents met.

☙

Tell your mother, "I love you mom!"
(Give her a hug and thank her for your life and being your mother.)

Cherish Sisters

Sisters can be very lovable and helpful. Sisters share your youthful experiences and often are good listeners. Sisters can be consoling or give constructive advice.

Sisters also help form our foundations for longer-term relationships. Sisters teach us how to share space, time and resources. (Do you recall getting ready for school and waiting your turn to shower without hot water? Do remember needing a few dollars to put gas in your car and your sister provided a loan until you got paid?)

Sisters share your parents and relatives. Sisters share in your love for them and any pain you may feel. Sisters share the laughter of family events and holidays. Sisters want you to love and be loved by special people. And sisters never want you to get hurt in relationships.

Never let your sister date one of your friends, unless he is twice the gentleman that you are.

☙

Hug your sister regularly after you become an adult.
(You will cherish her love because she can talk to you truthfully and still love you unconditionally.)

☙

Learn to laugh with your sister. You share a lifetime full of fun, tears, joy, pain, and similar DNA.

☙

Reminisce about the good old days.
(You'll discover that even though she played pranks on you, she also told girls that you were a pretty nice person.)

Protect your sister against all enemies inside and outside of your neighborhood.

꽃

If you get your driver's license before your sister and you have a car, allow her to drive it from time to time.

꽃

Find ways to give your sister what she ***wants*** and still get what **you need**.
(This principle will teach you how to develop win-win situations in the future.)

꽃

Ask your sister to teach you how to cook simple meals.
(She will be happy to tell her girlfriends how well you can cook. It will also come in handy when you cook for other special women in your life.)

Cherish Sisters

Avoid dating your sister's girlfriends. It puts a strain on her friendships when you end your relationships with them.

❧

Ask each sister what girls like and dislike. Their responses will provide valuable insights about women, their different styles and desires, thus paying dividends in your future.
(You will also appreciate and discover the diversities of the female gender.)

❧

Encourage your sister to have goals and dreams. Support and help her achieve them. When she achieves them, be one of the first to congratulate her and tell her that you knew she could do it.
(She will appreciate your loyalty and motivation.)

Become a good listener when your sister wants to talk to you about her future marriage. It may be hard to accept that she is getting married and you may also feel like you are losing her, but you will both adjust. Then you will become confidantes who share more than parents and sibling rivalries.

❧

I am proud to tell anyone that I have a sister. My sister really loves me, her big brother. When we were little, she always wanted to hug me. She still does it and I love her for it.

❧

Tell your sister, "I love you! We share parents, memories and a legacy." *(Embrace your similarities, respect your uniqueness and try to be friends.)*

Cherish Daughters

Daughters are like angels when they are born. Daughters are tiny, lovable and seem so innocent. Daughters have a glow that surrounds them and their smiles also carry a special warmth. Daughters often have a key to their daddy's heart and every tear shed feels like a needle pricking his heart.

Daughters are like dolls. Mothers enjoy shopping for their little girls. Mothers buy outfits in multiples and enjoy having daughters model each and every color and style. Later in life, daughters will grow into similar shoppers; sometimes, spending hours at this craft. Daughters develop their own unique sense of style for fashion.

Daughters will eventually share their sense of style and fashion with their friends. Daughters will adjust (or freely give their opinion of) the styles of the men in their life. This includes their boyfriends, father, husband, male friends and sons.

If the opportunity presents itself, be in the delivery room at the time of her birth. It will be the beginning of many miracles to follow and daily joys.

❧

Pour love into your child when they are mere babies and when they grow older, love will start flowing from them for a lifetime.
(Hold them, cuddle them, smile, laugh, blow on their tummies and make goofy faces. Tell her that she is mommy's or daddy's little girl or angel; children are a blessing to you.)

❧

Take pictures or videotape her activities. Include her taking her first steps or playing around the house, entertaining at family gatherings, holiday festivities, gymnastics workouts, brownies or girl scouts, plays or other like events.

Look into your daughter's eyes and see yourself.
(You helped create this life. Now, it's part of your responsibility to assist this little one to learn, grow and be happy.)

❧

While she is a little girl, take advantage of rainy days. Put on old, dirty clothes, boots and then go outside. Jump in the puddles with her.
(All of us know that a good puddle deserves to be splashed in.)

❧

Give her plenty of hugs and kisses while she's a little girl because her first words will be: "Da, Da!"

❧

Read her a story each night. Ham up the story. Give characters voices, show lots of facial expressions, and ask her to imitate those voices and expressions.
(It will add life and pizzazz to your stories.)

When she scrapes her knee or her heart is broken, tell her, "I'm sorry, but I know you are going to be OK."

🌿

Extend your arms to embrace your daughter daily and tell her, "I love you!" and "You are a good kid!" Do these simple tasks regardless of their good or bad deeds or their simple or complex days.
(We need to let them know that we will always love them.)

🌿

Take time to remember your little girl:

    a. Recall her smiling when you held her as a baby in your arms.
    b. Remember when she took her first steps.
    c. Remember when she called your name and ran into your arms.
    d. Remember the times when she was so very excited to show you her drawings of the family, the sun and the family home.
    e. Recall when her front teeth were missing. Did she smile or cover it when laughing?

Give your wife hugs and kisses in front of your daughter. Include her in family hugs.
(It shows that men and families can be affectionate.)

❧

While she is little, enjoy the magical moments like having tea with her and playing with her dolls, but never eat her mud pies.

❧

Apologize when you have done something wrong that affects her. She will then realize that, while fathers are not perfect; they can be strong and humble.

Buy your daughter some frilly outfits. Ask her to model them, and rave about how well she looks in them to build her self-esteem.

❧

Make sure your daughter is adorable for school dances and activities. She will spend many hours preparing for these special nights. Reassure her that she is pretty inside and out.

❧

Tell her, "I love you!" or, "I think you're a pretty, nice kid!" or, "I think you're special; and, when you grow up, someone else is going to believe you're special too!" or, "I am proud of you."
(She needs to hear you say that you love her and you have confidence in her.)

Teach her to mow the lawn, trim the bushes and paint the house.
(She will need these skills when she gets her first home.)

๑

Share your favorite recipes and show her how to prepare them, whether its barbecued ribs, smoked salmon, marinated steaks or shrimp kabobs.
(She'll have the special key to many men's hearts or should I say stomachs.)

๑

Attend her fun events like tumbling, gymnastics, swimming, plays, sporting events, car washes and graduations.
(She will look for you in the crowd and acknowledge you with a smile.)

Cherish Daughters

Teach her to save and invest a portion of all the money she receives. Learning to be financially responsible is an important lesson in life. *(Then she will have money for the everyday expenses and the big purchases like vacations, cars and homes.)*

ം

Try to be the best man, husband and father you can be. She is always watching you. And, one day, she will select a husband who resembles your good character, integrity and standards.

ം

As she becomes a teenager, try to be understanding. She is developing mentally and physically, which can be a very emotionally trying time for her and you.

Be patient with her during her teenage years. While you may already know the answers to her difficult situations, she may want to discover them without your assistance.

❦

Be accepting of her friends, both male and female. They are her friends and she will learn to be a good judge of character, morals and principles.
(Ask questions to keep the communication lines open, and be supportive.)

❦

Be understanding that she might not take the path that you have chosen or want her to choose. Sometimes, we want what we think is best for her and often feel that she does not have the experience to make the best choices.
(Support her choices and she will gain experience; you will gain her confidence and loyalty.)

Start communicating with her while she is a little girl. Talk to her about her day, events, teachers, friends and activities. As she matures, be sure to warn her about illegal drugs, premarital sex and young men's desires.

☙

The first young man who has the honor of dating your daughter should be pulled aside before the first date and given a stern talk and warning. Emphasize the treatment you expect of him, warn him that if he does mess up; you will have to clean up. And finally, tell **them** what time you expect them home.

☙

Trust your daughter. If you have communicated with her, she knows what you expect. She has also developed her own set of values and morals. You must believe that she will make the right choices at the right time.

Watch your daughter role play or interact with others. She will display your style and mannerisms. She will even use your exact words in certain situations.--- Know that she has always listened to you!

🌀

<u>Remember:</u> Only your children can honestly say whether or not you are a good father or mother. *(It doesn't matter what people outside of your family think or say. Always give her your best.)*

🌀

Daughters play a unique role in your life. They start out as little girls who sometimes carry our hearts on their sleeves. Then they grow into young women, who have children who will ultimately carry your legacy into the future. -- Cherish her joy, uniqueness and laughter.

There are times for reminiscing:

- Do you remember when she ran into your arms for protection?
- Do you remember when she rode her bicycle while you held the seat? Then one day, you let go of the seat and she rode by herself.
- Do you remember when she asked your opinion about everything?

When she grows older, she will become stronger and more mature, accepting challenges willingly, and, best of all, she will be able to make good decisions and work through the bad ones she makes.
(Subconsciously, give yourself a standing ovation and say, "Well done!")

Final Thoughts

As you think about the wonderful women who have graced your life, I hope you feel blessed and honored. Every relationship that you have encountered with women has had a purpose in building the foundation for your life. Even when the outcomes of relationships are not positive, there are still valuable lessons learned that will help you grow.

Ultimately, I believe that communication is the most important tool that we have in showing special people that we care. The women in your life need to know that you care and when you deliberately focus on your daughter, sister, mother, girlfriend or wife, only then can you see how gracefully and passionately they have or will enrich your life.

Final Thoughts

When I was becoming a young man, I wondered what it would be like to be rich. *(As I have experienced life, I found a wife, mother, aunt, daughter, sister and friends whom I consider my treasure. I am rich.)*

☙

Blessings arrive in tiny packages: our baby girls.
Blessings help us grow: our sisters.
Blessings provide us with understanding: our mothers and aunts.
Blessings help us to achieve our dreams: our wives and girlfriends.
Blessings come from God: God is good!

At the end of each day, I have a talk with God:

I thank God for the gift of these women in my life.
I thank God for blessing me with them, and I pray that
He will watch over them every day and night.
I pray for their happiness when life is going well.
I pray for their comfort when sorrow enters their lives.
I pray for their resilience to bounce back from bad times.
I pray for their tenacity to attain their goals that will make
their lives more wonderful.
And finally, I ask God to bless and keep them always!

Cherish Her
Quick Order Form

If you would like to order copies of the book "Cherish Her", you may place an order via email: http:www.CherishHer.com or place an order by mailing the form below to: High Point Publications, PO Box 2629, Olympia, WA 98507-2629. USA

Please send ___ copies of the book "Cherish Her". I understand that I may return any books ordered for a full refund – for any reason with no questions asked.

Address of shipment:

Name: _____
Address: _____
City: _____ State: ____ Zip Code: _____-_____
Telephone: _____
Email address: _____

Sales Tax: Please add 8.4% for products shipped to Washington addresses.

Shipping by air:
US: $4 for the first book and $2.00 for each additional product
International: $9 for first book and $5 for each additional product

Payment: Cashier's Check /Money Order or Credit Card:

Visa   MasterCard

Card number: _____

Name on Card: _____ Exp. Date: ____/_____